WHAT ON EARTH IS A
Nudibranch

JENNY TESAR

A BLACKBIRCH PRESS BOOK

WOODBRIDGE, CONNECTICUT

Published by Blackbirch Press, Inc.
One Bradley Road, Suite 104
Woodbridge, CT 06525

©1995 Blackbirch Press, Inc.
First Edition

Printed in the United States

10 9 8 7 6 5 4 3 2 1

Photo credits

Cover, title page: ©Fred Bavendam/Peter Arnold, Inc.
Pages 4—5: ©Bruce Watkins/Animals Animals; page 6: ©W. Gregory Brown/Animals Animals; page 7 (top): ©Bruce Watkins/Animals Animals; page 7 (bottom): ©Zig Leszczynski/Animals Animals; pages 8—9: ©Norbert Wu/Peter Arnold, Inc.; page 11: ©Doug Wechsler/Animals Animals; page 11 (inset): ©Scott Johnson/Animals Animals; pages 12—13: ©Captain Clay H. Wiseman/Animals Animals; pages 14—15: ©Peter Parks/Oxford Scientific Films/Animals Animals; page 15 (inset): ©Fred Bavendam/Peter Arnold, Inc.; page 16: ©Kathie Atkinson/Oxford Scientific Films/Animals Animals; pages 18—19: ©Fred Bavendam/Peter Arnold, Inc.; page 20: ©Zig Leszczynski/Animals Animals; page 21: ©Fred Bavendam/Peter Arnold, Inc.; page 23: ©Rodie Kuiter/Oxford Scientific Films/Animals Animals; page 24: ©Howard Hall/Oxford Scientific Films/Animals Animals; page 27: ©Scott Johnson/Animals Animals; pages 28—29: ©Peter Parks/Oxford Scientific Films/Animals Animals.

Library of Congress Cataloging-in-Publication Data
Tesar, Jenny E.
What on earth is a nudibranch? / by Jenny Tesar. — 1st ed.
    p.   cm. — (What on earth series)
    Includes bibliographical references (p.   ) and index.
    ISBN 1-56711-099-1 (lib. bdg.)
    1. Nudibranchia—Juvenile literature.   [1. Sea slugs.   2. Marine animals.]
I. Title.   II. Series.
QL430.4.T46   1995
594'.36—dc20   94-36826
                                                                      CIP
                                                                      AC

What does it look like?

Where does it live?

What does it eat?

How does it reproduce?

How does it survive?

TURN THESE PAGES AND FIND OUT!

A nudibranch is a beautiful little animal that lives in the sea. It is closely related to snails and slugs. In fact, nudibranchs are sometimes called sea slugs. But, unlike most of the slugs on land, nudibranchs are dazzling! Their bodies may be decorated with brightly colored stripes and dots. They may have showy extensions on their bodies that look like leaves, fringes, and knobs.

Scientists have identified about 2,500 different kinds, or species, of nudibranchs. Most species are no bigger than your thumb. Many are shorter than your smallest fingernail.

NUDIBRANCHS, OR SEA SLUGS, ARE COLORFUL ANIMALS THAT LIVE IN THE SEA.

Nudibranchs—like snails and slugs—belong to a group of animals called mollusks. Clams, oysters, and octopuses are also mollusks. The name *mollusk* comes from a Latin word meaning "soft." All mollusks have soft bodies. Most mollusks have hard shells that protect their soft bodies. Adult nudibranchs (and octopuses) do not have shells.

OPPOSITE: A
GREEN-GILL
NUDIBRANCH IS
ONE OF MANY
DIFFERENT
NUDIBRANCH
SPECIES.
LIKE THE
NUDIBRANCH, THE
OCTOPUS (TOP)
AND THE OYSTER
(BOTTOM) ARE
MOLLUSKS.

The name *nudibranch* comes from Greek and Latin words meaning "naked gills." Gills are organs that remove oxygen from the water—just like your lungs remove oxygen from the air. Some nudibranchs have gills on the outside of their body, where they are not covered by protective tissues. Other nudibranchs do not have gills. Some take in oxygen through gill-like organs called cerata and some take in oxygen through their skin.

A MULTICOLORED SPANISH-SHAWL NUDIBRANCH USES ITS BRIGHT ORANGE CERATA TO TAKE IN OXYGEN FROM THE WATER.

Nudibranchs have a wide variety of body shapes. They range in length from less than half an inch (1 centimeter) to nearly 2 feet (61 centimeters). All nudibranchs, however, have many features in common. On the head of most nudibranchs are two pairs of long tentacles, which are like antennae. These have sense organs that gather information about the nudibranch's surroundings. For example, one pair of tentacles, called rhinophores, can detect chemicals given off by nearby animals.

A nudibranch has a tongue called a radula. The radula is covered with many tiny teeth. As a nudibranch feeds, the radula scrapes back and forth like a file, loosening particles that can then be carried into the mouth. Worn-out and broken teeth are continuously replaced throughout the nudibranch's life.

On the underside of the nudibranch's body is a fleshy, muscular structure called the foot. The nudibranch uses its foot to swim, to creep over the ocean bottom, and to plow through sand.

NUDIBRANCHS USE THE SENSE ORGANS ON THEIR TENTACLES TO SENSE THEIR HABITAT. A KUNIE'S NUDIBRANCH (INSET) USES ITS FOOT TO CRAWL ACROSS ALGAE.

Nudibranchs live in all the oceans of the world. They even live in icy waters near the North and South poles. They are most common, however, in tropical and temperate (warmer) waters. Most nudibranch species live on coral reefs and on ocean bottoms close to shore. They move slowly over coral, rocks, and seaweed, or burrow between grains of sand.

A few kinds of nudibranchs do not live on the ocean bottom. They spend their entire lives on— or near—the water's surface. There, they float upside down or attach themselves to jellyfish.

A BLUEBERRY NUDIBRANCH CREEPS ALONG THE FLOOR OF THE PACIFIC OCEAN.

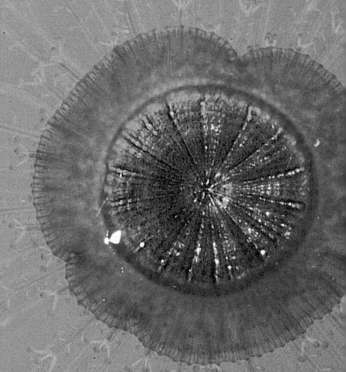

Nudibranchs are carnivores, or meat-eaters. They catch and eat other animals. Nudibranchs do not have eyes. They find food mostly by touch. Once they capture their prey, they use their jaws to hold onto the animal while their radula scrapes off particles.

Nudibranchs feed on sea anemones, sponges, worms, barnacles, and even small fish. Many nudibranchs feed on jellyfish and small jellyfish-like animals called hydroids.

ABOVE: A GIANT NUDIBRANCH
ATTACKS A SEA ANEMONE.

WHILE FLOATING IN WATER,
A NUDIBRANCH FEEDS ON A
JELLYFISH.

A SPECTACULAR, BUTTERFLY-LIKE NUDIBRANCH NESTLES IN A BED
OF SEAWEED.

A nudibranch's ocean world is filled with life. Fish and jellyfish swim about. Crabs and sea stars creep along the ocean's bottom. Worms and clams hide under rocks and plants.

Seaweeds are a very important part of the ocean world. Like green plants on land, seaweeds can make their own food. Animals cannot make food. They must eat seaweeds and other organisms in order to survive.

Many hungry animals try to eat nudibranchs. But nudibranchs protect themselves with some very good defenses.

Young fish gulp down nudibranchs without hesitation. But, within seconds, they spit them out. Lobsters and crabs also nibble on nudibranchs, but quickly stop. After a few bites, they learn to leave the nudibranchs alone.

This is because some nudibranchs produce acids that make them taste awful. Others produce deadly poisons. Nudibranchs that eat hydroids can actually defend themselves with weapons taken from those hydroids.

Hydroids have special stinging cells. Many animals avoid hydroids because of these stinging cells, but nudibranchs can eat hydroids without being harmed. When a nudibranch eats a hydroid, some of the stinging cells pass into the colorful, fleshy cerata on the nudibranch's back. Later, when another animal tries to eat the nudibranch, it gets blasted by the stinging cells.

A RED-GILLED NUDIBRANCH DINES ON A HYDROID. AFTER IT IS EATEN, THE HYDROID'S STINGING CELLS BECOME PART OF THE NUDIBRANCH'S BODY.

A GREEN CARIBBEAN RIBBON NUDIBRANCH IS CAMOUFLAGED WITHIN ITS GREEN SURROUNDINGS.

In addition to acids, poisons, and "borrowed" stinging cells, nudibranchs have other effective defenses for survival. Some escape predators by jumping up and swimming away. Nudibranchs cannot swim very far or very fast, but their movements are often enough to get out of the way of a prowling starfish.

Other nudibranchs depend on camouflage for protection. Camouflage means hiding by blending into the surroundings. Camouflaging nudibranchs will often turn the color of their food. A nudibranch that feeds on a blue jellyfish turns blue. One that feeds on a red sponge turns red.

THE ORANGE-PEEL NUDIBRANCH GETS ITS COLOR FROM THE ORANGE SEA PEN ON WHICH IT FEEDS.

Like all living things, nudibranchs must reproduce, or make more creatures of the same kind. Most animals are either male or female. Males produce reproductive cells called sperm. Females produce eggs. During reproduction, an egg and sperm combine, and the egg is said to be fertilized.

Unlike most animals, a nudibranch is both male and female. It produces both sperm and eggs. When two nudibranchs mate, they exchange sperm. The sperm of each nudibranch fertilizes the eggs of the other nudibranch.

TWO NUDIBRANCHS MATE ON THE OCEAN FLOOR.

A RAINBOW
NUDIBRANCH
ATTACHES ITS EGGS
TO A SOLID SURFACE
IN THE SEA.

After mating, a nudibranch sheds its fertilized eggs into the sea or attaches them to a hard surface. Nudibranch eggs have been found on seaweed, coral, empty shells, and floating bottles. Each species lays its eggs in a certain way. Some lay their eggs in long spiral ribbons. A nudibranch lays thousands of eggs at a time.

Nudibranch parents do not protect their eggs. Many of the eggs are eaten by hungry animals. That is why nudibranchs must produce so many eggs at once. Eggs that survive will hatch within a few days.

Baby nudibranchs do not look like their parents. They are born with shells, like other mollusks. Their bodies are covered with tiny hair-like structures that help them swim in the surface waters. Eventually, ocean currents may carry them far away from where they were born.

Young nudibranchs lose their shells soon after birth. After the shells are gone, a nudibranch's body gradually changes into the adult form.

Nudibranchs have short life spans. Most kinds live for only about a year.

THIS YOUNG NUDIBRANCH (RESTING INSIDE THE RIBBON OF EGGS)
LOOKS NOTHING LIKE THE ADULT NUDIBRANCH NEXT TO IT.

A SPANISH-DANCER
NUDIBRANCH COVERS A
DIVER'S FACE MASK.

Nudibranchs are very popular with people who enjoy diving and who like to explore tide pools. The nudibranch's bright colors and swaying movements fascinate many underwater explorers who like to watch and photograph these little animals.

But some actions of people kill and endanger nudibranchs. Garbage and other wastes that are dumped into oceans bury nudibranchs. And harmful chemicals dumped into oceans poison nudibranchs and other sea creatures. This upsets the balance of living things.

Many countries have created underwater parks along their shores. They have passed laws that protect tide pools and coral reefs from ocean dumping and other harmful activities. By protecting Earth's precious ocean resources, we also protect nudibranchs. This allows them to survive and captivate us for generations to come.

Glossary

camouflage The ability to blend into the surroundings.

carnivore An animal that eats meat.

cerata Fleshy extensions on a nudibranch's body.

fertilization The joining of a male sex cell, called a sperm, and a female sex cell, called an egg. Fertilization is a part of reproduction.

hydroids Small relatives of jellyfish that are eaten by many nudibranchs.

mollusks Soft-bodied animals that usually have hard shells. Clams, snails, slugs, and nudibranchs are examples of mollusks.

radula A nudibranch's tongue.

reproduction Making more creatures of the same kind.

rhinophores A pair of tentacles on a nudibranch's head that sense the presence of chemicals.

species A group of living things that are closely related to one another. Members of a species can reproduce with one another.

temperate A moderate climate; not very warm or very cold.

tentacles Long, thin structures on the nudibranch's head, used to sense changes in the environment.

Further Reading

Barrett, Norman. *Coral Reef*. New York: Watts, 1991.

Carlisle, Madelyn W. *Let's Investigate Weird and Wonderful Sea Creatures.* Happauge, NY: Barron, 1993.

Carwardine, Mark. *Water Animals*. Ada, OK: Garrett Educational Corp., 1989.

Chinery, Michael. *Ocean Animals*. New York: Random, 1992.

Coldrey, Jennifer. *Life in the Sea*. New York: Watts, 1989.

Downer, Ann. *Don't Blink Now! Capturing the Hidden World of Sea Creatures*. New York: Watts, 1991.

Kindersley, Dorling. *Sea Animals*. New York: Macmillan Child Group, 1992.

Richardson, Joy. *Mollusks*. New York: Watts, 1993.

Rinard, Judy. *Amazing Animals of the Sea*. Washington, D.C.: National Geographic, 1981.

Williams, Brian. *Under the Sea*. New York: Random, 1989.

Index